A Closer Look at BIOLOGY, MICROBIOLOGY, AND THE CELL

A Closer Look at BIOLOGY, MICROBIOLOGY, AND THE CELL

Edited by Sherman Hollar

Britannica
Educational Publishing
IN ASSOCIATION WITH
ROSEN
EDUCATIONAL SERVICES

Published in 2012 by Britannica Educational Publishing
(a trademark of Encyclopædia Britannica, Inc.)
in association with Rosen Educational Services, LLC
29 East 21st Street, New York, NY 10010.

AUG 2 3 2011

First Edition

Britannica Educational Publishing
Michael I. Levy: Executive Editor, Encyclopædia Britannica
J.E. Luebering: Director, Core Reference Group, Encyclopædia Britannica
Adam Augustyn: Assistant Manager, Encyclopædia Britannica

Anthony L. Green: Editor, Compton's by Britannica
Michael Anderson: Senior Editor, Compton's by Britannica
Sherman Hollar: Associate Editor, Compton's by Britannica

Marilyn L. Barton: Senior Coordinator, Production Control
Steven Bosco: Director, Editorial Technologies
Lisa S. Braucher: Senior Producer and Data Editor
Yvette Charboneau: Senior Copy Editor
Kathy Nakamura: Manager, Media Acquisition

Rosen Educational Services
Heather M. Moore Niver: Editor
Nelson Sá: Art Director
Cindy Reiman: Photography Manager
Karen Huang: Photo Researcher
Matthew Cauli: Designer, Cover Design
Introduction by Heather M. Moore Niver

Library of Congress Cataloging-in-Publication Data

A closer look at biology, microbiology, and the cell / edited by Sherman Hollar.—1st ed.
    p. cm.—(The Environment: Ours to Save)
"In association with Britannica Educational Publishing, Rosen Educational Services."
Includes bibliographical references and index.
ISBN 978-1-61530-514-8 (library binding)
1. Biology—Juvenile literature. 2. Microbiology—Juvenile literature. 3. Cells—Juvenile literature. I.
Hollar, Sherman.
QH309.2C56 2011
570—dc22

                                                                2011000401

Manufactured in the United States of America

On the cover (front and back), page 3: Red blood cells. *Shutterstock.com*

On the front cover: Hand holding test tubes. *Shutterstock.com*

Pages 18, 21, 22, 32, 33, 46, 55, 83, 84, 87, 90, 93, 94 © www.istockphoto.com/ChristianAnthony; remaining interior background images © www.istockphoto.com/Henrik Jonsson

CONTENTS

INTRODUCTION 6

CHAPTER 1 AREAS OF STUDY IN BIOLOGY 10

CHAPTER 2 HISTORY OF BIOLOGY 26

CHAPTER 3 THE FIELD OF MICROBIOLOGY 38

CHAPTER 4 CELL STRUCTURE AND FUNCTION 52

CHAPTER 5 HISTORY OF CELL THEORY 76

CONCLUSION 85
GLOSSARY 87
FOR MORE INFORMATION 90
BIBLIOGRAPHY 93
INDEX 94

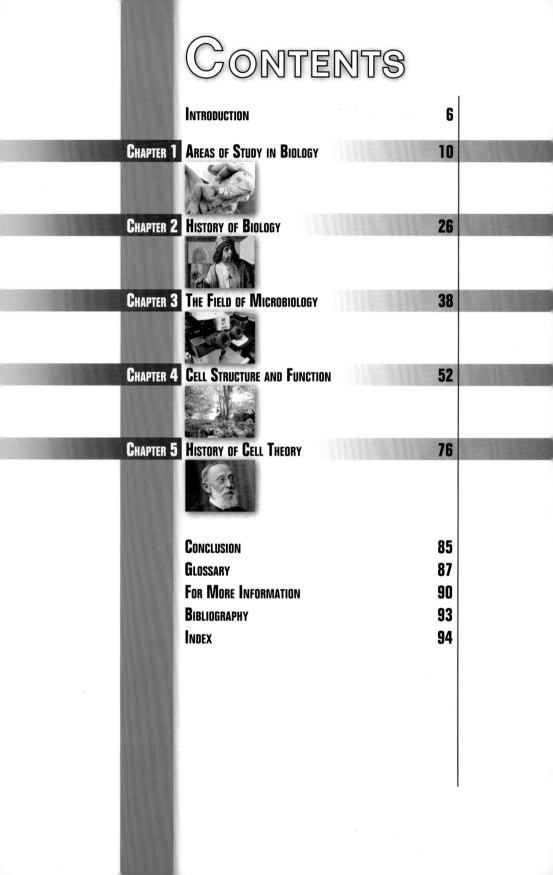

Plants, animals, fungi, protozoa, algae, bacteria, and viruses all inhabit the natural world. Biology is the study of these and other living things. Today's constantly advancing technology allows researchers to investigate nature's tiniest living organisms; this field of study is known as microbiology.

In this volume you will learn about many of the branches of biology. The sheer volume of scientific information available can be mind-boggling, but areas of specialization allow scientists to focus on certain areas, like animals (zoology) or plants (botany). Some biologists study even more specific areas, such as insects (entomology) or bacteria (bacteriology).

You will also learn about the history of biology. The early Greeks were the first to formally study the natural world. During the Renaissance, Leonardo da Vinci linked human anatomy to that of animals. Swedish biologist Carolus Linnaeus devised the modern method of classifying organisms, known as taxonomy.

The development of the microscope has been and continues to be a huge scientific advancement. Scientists began to develop microscopes as early as the 1600s. This powerful tool allowed them to study all kinds of previously unknown processes and structures, including the cell. Modern microscopes, in particular electron microscopes, have helped scientists unravel the mysteries of DNA.

Areas of microbiology you will read about include bacteriology, protozoology (the study of protozoans), phycology (algae), mycology (fungi), virology (viruses), and exobiology (life outside Earth). Some microbiologists have made great strides with pure cultures (cultures containing the growth of a single kind of organism free from other organisms) and methods of cultivating and identifying microbes.

You will also learn about the very unit that interests so many scientists: the cell. Some organisms, such as yeasts, are single-celled, but others, such as humans, are composed of many billions of cells. Simple cells only have a few parts, but more complex cells have a variety of parts with many functions.

Finally, you will learn about the rich history of cell theory. Robert Hooke first coined the term "cell" in the 1600s.

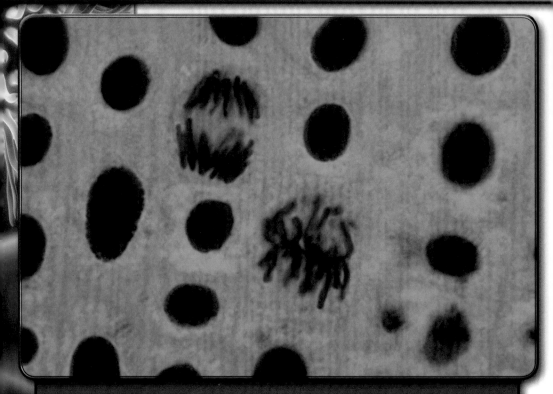

Cells reproduce through a process of division called mitosis. **Paul Zahl/ National Geographic Image Collection/Getty Images**

Scientists initially made slow progress in their studies and observations of cells. Anthony van Leeuwenhoek gave the first accurate description of red blood cells, but it was not until the 1800s—when better microscopes were available—that biologists could see details that proved cells contain living material.

Scientists also investigated the origin of cells. The theory of free cell formation, in which it was thought that cells developed from an unformed substance, persisted for many years. Eventually, Rudolph Virchow affirmed that all cells come from cells, but the complexities of cell division gave biologists pause. Walther Flemming's methods of fixing and staining cells revealed how chromosomes move from the parent to daughter cells by the process of mitosis. Subsequently, the discovery that the number of chromosomes remains constant from one generation to the next led to the full description of the process of meiosis.

Biologists continue to question how life around us occurs. The fields of biology and microbiology have produced many important discoveries, including the medicines and antibiotics that treat infections and illnesses every day. Much about the natural world remains a mystery, but persistent studies in these fields will lead toward a better understanding of living things and the environment that supports them.

CHAPTER 1

AREAS OF STUDY IN BIOLOGY

The scientific study of living things is called biology. Biologists strive to understand the natural world and its living inhabitants—plants, animals, fungi, protozoa, algae, bacteria, archaea, and viruses—by asking why and how the processes of life occur. Why do living organisms interact with each other in particular ways? When did they evolve? How are biological processes carried out within organs, tissues, and cells? To answer these broad questions, biologists must answer many specific ones: How does an animal's liver break down fat? How does a green plant convert water and carbon dioxide into sugar? Where do mosquitoes go in the winter?

Some investigations require years of scientific research. Today many mysteries remain unsolved, but continued study leads toward a better understanding of living things and the environment they depend on.

The annual output of biological research today is so massive that no single individual can possibly acquire all of the information. Because of this, areas of specialization have

Some biologists specialize in a single area, such as zoology. **Hemera Technologies/AbleStock.com/Thinkstock**

developed, allowing scientists to focus on their own research, yet remain informed on key developments in their fields.

Some biologists focus their research on one or several groups of organisms. Such specializations can be broad, such as zoology (the study of animals) and botany (the study of plants); or they can be specific, as in the following fields:

- Arachnology: spiders, mites, scorpions
- Bryology: mosses
- Entomology: insects
- Herpetology: reptiles and amphibians
- Ichthyology: fishes
- Mammalogy: mammals
- Microbiology: microscopic organisms
- Mycology: fungi
- Ornithology: birds
- Parasitology: parasites
- Phycology: algae
- Virology: viruses

Some biologists study specific features, such as structure, or explore broad biological concepts. Such studies often look for general principles that apply to different types of organisms. Some examples are:

- Anatomy: the structure of living things
- Cytology: cells
- Ethology: animal behavior
- Genetics: heredity
- Pathology: disease and its effect on the body
- Physiology: biological functions

Biologists may be identified by the group of organisms they study or by their area of research. For example, a scientist who studies nonhuman primates (such as apes and monkeys) is called a primatologist; a scientist who studies genetics is called a geneticist.

The following sections discuss a small fraction of the many specialized areas of biological research.

TAXONOMY

Naming organisms and establishing their relationships to one another comprise the field of taxonomy (also called systematics). Modern taxonomy is based on a system established in the 1750s by Swedish botanist Carolus Linnaeus.

The Linnaean system classifies organisms based on shared attributes and the closeness of their evolutionary relationships. The most basic category is the species (spelled identically for both singular and plural forms). Individual members of a species share common characteristics and a closer genetic relationship with each other than they share with members of other species. The next highest taxon (level of organization) is the

Carolus Linnaeus. Hulton Archive/Getty Images

genus (plural: genera), which includes groups of related species.

All species have a two-part scientific name. The first part is the genus, or generic, name. For example, wolves and coyotes belong to the same genus: *Canis*. The second part of the name is the specific name: wolves are members of the species *Canis lupus*, while coyotes belong to the species *Canis latrans*. The whole scientific name is always italicized; the generic name is capitalized, while the specific name is not.

The relatedness between groups within a taxon becomes increasingly distant at higher levels: genera with similar traits are grouped into the same "family"; related families are classified in the same "order"; related orders are placed into the same "class"; related classes are placed in the same "phylum"; related phyla (plural of phylum) are placed into a "kingdom"; and related kingdoms are placed into a "domain," the highest level of classification. The higher taxonomic levels indicate phylogenetic relationships—the degree to which species have diverged from each other during the course of evolution.

The classification of living things is frequently challenged and revised. Taxonomic studies may be based on morphological (structural) traits, such as skull shape and jaw length, or on molecular data, such as DNA, RNA, or protein sequences.

EMBRYOLOGY AND DEVELOPMENTAL BIOLOGY

Developmental biologists examine the processes that control the growth and development of organisms. Included within the field are studies of embryological development of plants or animals and the natural phenomenon of regeneration in which removed cells, tissues, or entire structures of an organism grow back. Research in development has direct applications for agriculture and for human and veterinary medicine. An example of this is cloning, in which cells from an adult plant or animal are used to grow a genetically identical individual. Plant cloning is widely used in agriculture and horticulture. Several types of animals, such as sheep, cows, and cats, have been cloned, though the practice is not widespread. Stem cell research is another example of developmental biology. The capability of stem cells (cells in extremely

Although cloning and stem cell research show a great deal of medical promise, their use remains controversial. Peter Dazeley/ Photographer's Choice/Getty Images

early stages of development) to grow many different kinds of living tissue in laboratory cultures has broad potential in medicine. Despite their potential in medicine, however, cloning and stem cell research remain controversial.

17

Bioethics

Biology and medicine are sciences, and they both deal with living beings. They have direct effects on human beings and other living species, so they quickly raise ethical and other value problems as well as scientific ones. Bioethics is the branch of ethics, or moral decision-making, that deals with the problems of biology and medicine. It requires disciplined, systematic reflection on these difficult issues.

Scientists can change the genetic information in bacteria and are rapidly developing the capacity to change it in many animal species, including humans. But should they? People change the nature of the human population by aborting defective or unwanted fetuses, controlling when pregnancy occurs, and planning limits on population size. But should they? Physicians can keep seriously ill patients alive indefinitely, using artificial respirators, machines that take over the control of the beating of the heart, and drugs to control blood pressure and consciousness. But should they?

People are beginning to ask whether there comes a time when patients should be allowed to die. Citizens are claiming "patients' rights," insisting on being informed about medical procedures and deciding how to allocate health resources fairly. When they ask these questions and make these decisions, they are dealing with bioethics.

ANATOMY AND MORPHOLOGY

Anatomists study the structure of organisms. Some morphological research compares homologous (similar in origin) or analogous (similar in function) structures among different species to establish phylogenetic relationships. Other studies may investigate the function or mode of operation of an anatomical feature. Histology (study of tissues) and cytology (study of cells) are specialized areas of morphology.

PHYSIOLOGY

A physiologist studies the functions of organs and tissues. A cell physiologist investigates processes at the subcellular level. Animal or plant physiologists may study entire systems, such as circulatory or respiratory. Many physiological studies are intimately associated with morphology.

GENETICS AND MOLECULAR BIOLOGY

Molecular biology and genetics are two of the most dynamic fields of biology today.

New laboratory techniques developed during the 20th century allowed scientists to examine the structure and function of biological molecules, such as DNA and proteins, and determine their relationship to cellular structures, such as the nucleus and cell membrane. Geneticists also have benefited from molecular studies on genes and chromosomes. However, the use of genetic engineering in medicine and agriculture has raised many new moral and philosophical issues.

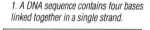

1. A DNA sequence contains four bases linked together in a single strand.

DNA Bases

adenine A — T thymine
guanine G — C cytosine

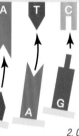

2. Complementary bases join together following base pairing rules.

3. Complementary bases bond together, forming a double-stranded molecule of DNA

DNA contains two strands of nucleotides linked together by chemical bonds. Each nucleotide contains a phosphate, deoxyribose (a sugar), and one of four nitrogen-containing bases—adenine (A), guanine (G), cytosine (C), or thymine (T). The bases of one strand are linked to bases of the second strand. Because of their structures, adenine can only pair with thymine, and cytosine can only pair with guanine. Encyclopædia Britannica, Inc.

GENETIC ENGINEERING

Almost every living cell holds a vast storehouse of information encoded in genes, segments of DNA that control how the cell replicates and functions and the expression of inherited traits. The artificial manipulation of one or more genes to modify an organism is called genetic engineering.

The term "genetic engineering" initially encompassed all the methods used for modifying organisms through heredity and reproduction. These included selective breeding, or artificial selection, as well as a wide range of biomedical techniques such as artificial insemination, in vitro fertilization, and gene manipulation. Today, however, the term is used to refer to the latter technique, specifically the field of recombinant DNA technology. In this process DNA molecules from two or more sources are combined and then inserted into a host organism, such as a bacterium. Inside the host cell the inserted, or foreign, DNA replicates and functions along with the host DNA.

Recombinant DNA technology has produced many new genetic combinations that have greatly affected science, medicine, agriculture, and industry. Despite the tremendous advances afforded to society through this technology, however, the practice is not without controversy. Special concern has been focused on the use of microorganisms in recombinant technology, with the worry that some genetic changes could introduce unfavorable and possibly dangerous traits, such as antibiotic resistance or toxin production, into microbes that were previously free of these.

ECOLOGY

Ecologists study the relationships and interactions between organisms and their environments by examining the structure and function of ecosystems. Many ecological studies require input from other scientific disciplines, such as geology, animal behavior, and botany. Policy makers and scientists interested in conservation issues need a solid understanding of ecology to understand how changes such as pollution and habitat destruction affect natural communities at both the local and the global level.

ETHOLOGY AND SOCIOBIOLOGY

Ethologists, or animal behaviorists, attempt to understand why animals behave the way they do. Some studies involve direct

Ethologist Jane Goodall. Fotos International/Archive Photos/ Getty Images

observations of animals in their native habitats, while others may involve experiments using laboratory animals. Ethology is tied closely to the fields of psychology and sociology. Sociobiology is concerned with the social interactions within a given species and focuses on such issues as whether certain traits, such as intelligence, are inherited or are culturally induced.

Paleontology (the study of fossils) can be a useful tool for many evolutionary biologists. **Photodisc/Thinkstock**

EVOLUTIONARY BIOLOGY

The evolution of species by natural selection is considered by the great majority of biologists to be a fundamental tenet of modern biology. Evolutionary biology seeks to answer questions about the origin and the genetic relationships of all living things. Some evolutionary biologists examine genetic relationships by comparing DNA sequences,

24

while others may compare structural features or physiology. Many evolutionary biologists use knowledge gleaned from paleontology (the study of fossils).

OTHER AREAS OF STUDY

Although the aforementioned categories represent the major subdivisions of biology, there are many other research areas. Some are based on life in specific environments. Marine biology, for example, looks at many aspects of ocean life, whereas soil biology focuses on organisms and processes occurring in soil.

Many other scientific disciplines also require knowledge of biology. For example, biochemistry, a subdivision of organic chemistry, focuses on subcellular chemical processes and requires a solid foundation in cell biology.

CHAPTER 2

HISTORY OF BIOLOGY

No one knows precisely when humans first began to acquire knowledge of the natural world. Most experts believe that humans had been domesticating many animals and cultivating crops long before written records were kept. The earliest records show that the Assyrians and Babylonians had some knowledge of agriculture and medicine as early as 3500 BC. By 2500 BC this knowledge was widely applied by the major civilizations of China, Egypt, and India.

THE GREEKS AND NATURAL LAW

The early Greeks were the first to formally investigate and describe the natural world. The concepts of cause and effect and that of a natural law that governs the universe were proposed around 600 BC. Some 200 years later, the Greek physician Hippocrates observed among other things the effect of the environment on human nature.

In the mid-4th century BC Aristotle presented the first system for classifying animals

Aristotle. **Photos.com/Thinkstock**

based on similarity of structure and function. His student Theophrastus drew up a scheme for classifying many of the plants. The writings of Galen, a Greek physician who lived in Rome during the 2nd century AD, influenced medicine for hundreds of years.

THE MIDDLE AGES

During the Middle Ages (roughly AD 500–1400), the center of biological studies shifted from Europe to the Middle East. The Islamic scholar al-Jahiz expanded on the observations of the Greeks. His multi-volume *Book of Animals* discussed a variety of topics, such as the relationships among different animal groups and animal mimicry. The writings of the Persian physician Avicenna (Ibn Sina), based on the observations of Aristotle, helped revive European interest in biology.

A REBIRTH OF SCIENTIFIC LEARNING

Major biological advancements were made in Europe during the Renaissance (about AD 1300 to 1650). The serious study of anatomy emerged in the 1500s through the efforts of Leonardo da Vinci and Andreas Vesalius, who documented the relationships between the anatomies of humans and of other animals. Advances in anatomy and physiology were made by means of dissection of organisms during the 16th and 17th centuries.

Prior to the 16th century, it was commonly believed that organisms such as flies and worms arose from mud or other inanimate substrates. Although some scientists had previously disputed this idea of spontaneous generation, the concept remained untested. In 1668 the Italian physician Francesco Redi was the first to challenge the concept using a set of controlled experiments.

Interest in botany also increased during the 16th and 17th centuries.

Francesco Redi. **De Agostini Picture Library/Getty Images**

Numerous papers published by botanists such as Otto Brunfels of Germany and Gaspard Bauhin of Switzerland discussed horticulture and other plant-related topics.

Replica of Robert Hooke's compound microscope. The 17th-century invention and development of the microscope revealed unknown processes and organisms. **Dave King/Dorling Kindersley/Getty Images**

DEVELOPMENT OF THE MICROSCOPE

The invention and development of the microscope in the 1600s generated an explosion of interest in biological studies. The value of this important new research tool was phenomenal. Unsuspected processes and organisms unknown to science were discovered in a flurry of biological investigation. Anthony van Leeuwenhoek reported his observations of single-celled animal-like creatures (protozoa) invisible to the naked eye. He subsequently observed spermatozoa, leading to new questions and interpretations of the male role in fertilization and reproduction.

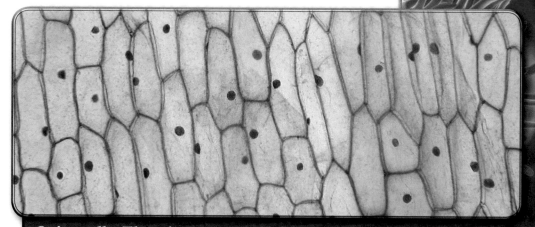

Onion cells. The microscope enabled Robert Hooke to observe tiny compartments he called "cells." Shutterstock.com

Anthony van Leeuwenhoek

By means of his extraordinary ability to grind lenses, Anthony van Leeuwenhoek greatly improved the microscope as a scientific tool. This led to his doing a vast amount of innovative research on bacteria, protozoa, and other small life-forms that he called "animalcules" (tiny animals).

Leeuwenhoek was born in Delft, Holland, on Oct. 24, 1632. He probably did not have much scientific education because his family could not afford it. He first became a haberdasher (a dealer in men's clothing and accessories) and draper (a dealer in cloth or clothing and dry goods) and, in 1660, chamberlain to the sheriffs at Delft. His hobby was lens grinding. In his lifetime he ground about 400 lenses, most of which were quite small, with a magnifying power of from 50 to 300 times.

It was not only his lenses that made him world famous but also his work with the microscope. His keen powers of observation led to discoveries of major significance. For example, he observed and calculated the sizes of bacteria and protozoa and gave the first accurate description of red blood cells.

Although Leeuwenhoek lived in Delft, he maintained a regular correspondence with the Royal Society of England, to which he was elected in 1680. Most of his discoveries were published in the society's *Philosophical Transactions*. He continued his work throughout most of his 90 years. He died in Delft on Aug. 26, 1723.

The concept of cells was introduced in 1665, when the English physicist Robert Hooke reported on the presence of tiny compartments in tissue he was studying under a microscope. Hooke named the compartments "cells." Marcello Malpighi used the microscope to observe and describe many microscopic structures, including red blood cells. Many other contributions to biology were made during this period as a result of discoveries in this previously unseen microscopic world.

BIOLOGICAL CLASSIFICATION

The publication in the 1750s of Carolus Linnaeus' biological classification scheme for organisms was a major advance in biology. Linnaeus was one of the first taxonomists to organize living things in a simple and logical manner, using a system of binomial nomenclature (two-part names) that appealed to most scientists. The Linnaean system indicates both the degree of similarity and difference among species, and it persists today as the basis for naming living things.

EVOLUTIONARY THEORY

New biological theories developed rapidly during the 18th and 19th centuries and challenged many old ideas. The British naturalist Charles Darwin published his theory about evolution in the book *On the Origin of Species by Means of Natural Selection* (1859). Darwin's ideas centered around observations he had made in the Galápagos Islands, an archipelago off the coast of Ecuador. Another British naturalist, Alfred Russel Wallace, made similar observations about animals in Indonesia, and the research of both scientists was presented simultaneously to their peers. Although Darwin's efforts received wider attention, Wallace's observations about the geographic distribution of plants and animals remain vital in modern studies of evolution.

The concept of natural selection and evolution revolutionized 19th-century thinking about the relationships between groups of plants and animals and about speciation (the origin of new species). Darwin provided sound scientific reasoning for the wealth of biological variability and similarity that exists among living things. Although genetics and the mechanisms of inheritance were unknown during Darwin's time, he noted that certain life forms were more likely to survive than others, and proposed that this was influenced by variable traits (such as beak size in birds) that were passed from parents to offspring. This concept of natural selection provided the first scientific explanation of the variations observed in nature. Darwin also proposed that new species are formed—and others become extinct—by a gradual process of change and adaptation made possible by this natural variability. Although Darwin's ideas provoked tremendous controversy, they influenced biology more than any other concept and today are generally accepted by the scientific community.

MECHANISM OF HEREDITY

The mechanism that produced the heritable variation needed for natural selection was discovered in the mid-19th century by Gregor Mendel. An Austrian monk interested in plant breeding, Mendel's experiments with garden peas revealed that the peas inherited characteristics from their parents in a mathematically predictable fashion. His findings

Gregor Mendel studied the blossoms of garden peas and proved the mathematical foundation of the science of genetics, in what came to be called Mendelism. Shutterstock.com

introduced the concept of the gene as the unit of inheritance, or heredity. Although Mendel published his results in 1866, the significance of his studies remained obscure until 1900. The rediscovery of Mendel's work and the discovery of chromosomes in the early 20th century spurred development of studies of genetics and heredity and strengthened science's understanding of evolution.

MODERN DEVELOPMENTS

An important milestone in the history of biology was the discovery in 1953 of the structure of DNA and the subsequent unraveling of the genetic code of life. These discoveries aided science's understanding of genetic diseases in plants and animals and allowed for unprecedented discoveries in molecular biology. Advances in the technology for copying and manipulating DNA ushered in the age of biotechnology with practical applications in agriculture, industry, and medicine. It also enabled efforts to decipher the entire genetic code (genome) of many organisms. As genetic sequencing became faster and less expensive, it spurred biological research in such areas as the study of gene expression and function in biological processes.

Some developments had negative effects on the natural world, however. Increased urbanization and industrialization destroyed many habitats and threatened the existence of countless species, while pollution and the emergence of new infectious diseases such as AIDS endangered public health. The growth of biotechnology also raised concerns over its potential hazards to health and the environment and the need to monitor and regulate its use.

CHAPTER 3

THE FIELD OF MICROBIOLOGY

Scientific exploration to understand the nature of the tiniest living organisms constitutes the field of microbiology. Such organisms are known as microbes, and the scientists who study them are called microbiologists.

Over the years, microbiology has extended to include more than microbes alone. For instance, the field of immunology, which studies the body's reaction to microbes, is closely aligned with microbiology. In addition, a whole new field of molecular biology has emerged. Today molecular biologists study the properties of cellular structures such as proteins and nucleic acids.

Microbes are widely spread over the surface of the Earth and play a crucial role in ecology. Soil and water contain high concentrations of bacteria and molds (two types of microbes), and the surface of every human body is covered with a unique microbial flora. Certain bacteria draw nitrogen from the air and pass it on to plants in the soil. Others help break down and recycle organic materials and waste products.

The action caused by yeast microbes makes bread dough rise.
Shutterstock.com

The action of microbes has also been harnessed for industrial uses. Yeast is used in the production of bread and alcohol. Other microscopic organisms are used for the production of many foodstuffs and for the degradation of industrial by-products. The research and development of microbes for such practical uses is the subject of applied microbiology.

Areas of Study

Microbiologists classify microorganisms into bacteria, protozoans, algae, fungi, and viruses, and the study of each constitutes a separate specialty within microbiology. Individual fields may overlap, and the discipline of microbiology may overlap with other disciplines, as it does with immunology. In any case, most areas of scientific inquiry can be subdivided in a variety of ways, depending on the questions being asked. Microbiology may be subdivided as follows.

Bacteriology

The study of bacteria is called bacteriology. Bacteria are single-cell microbes that grow in nearly every environment on Earth. They are used to study disease and produce antibiotics, to ferment foods, to make chemical solvents, and in many other applications.

Protozoology

Protozoology is the study of protozoans, small single-cell microbes. They are frequently observed as actively moving organisms when impure water is viewed under a microscope. Protozoans cause a number of widespread human illnesses, such as malaria, and thus can present a threat to public health.

PHYCOLOGY AND MYCOLOGY

Phycologists study algae. In general, algae are organisms that are made up of one or more eukaryotic cells (cells with a true nucleus) that contain chlorophyll and that are less complex than plants. Mycology is the study of fungi—well-known organisms that lack chlorophyll, as well as the organized plant structures of stems, roots, and leaves. Fungi usually derive food and energy from parasitic growth on dead organisms.

VIROLOGY

Viruses are a vastly different kind of biological entity. They are the smallest form of replicating microbe. Viruses are never free-living; they must enter living cells to grow. Thus they are considered by most microbiologists to be nonliving. There is an infectious virus for almost every known

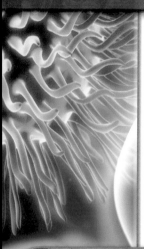

kind of cell. Viruses are visible only with the most powerful microscopes, namely electron microscopes.

EXOBIOLOGY

Exobiology is the study of life outside the Earth, including that on other planets. Space probes have been sent to Mars, and samples

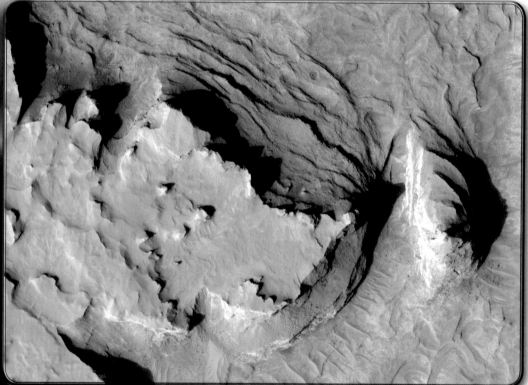

Exobiologists search for traces of microbial life in rock samples from Mars and other planets. NASA/JPL-Caltech/University of Arizona

of rocks have been brought back from our moon as part of experiments to search for traces of microbial life in extraterrestrial environments. Most exobiologists examine such samples for the basic building blocks of life known to have evolved on Earth. Because microbes were probably the earliest organisms on Earth, and because they have continued to thrive, exobiologists consider microbes to be the most likely form of life to exist beyond the Earth.

BIOLOGICAL WARFARE

Another area of study in microbiology involves the development, deployment, and defense against agents of biological warfare. Both chemical and biological agents have been used in past wars because they are often more insidious and less easily detected than conventional weapons. This application of microbiology has been made still more ominous by the ability to alter microbes using genetic engineering.

METHODS OF MICROBIOLOGY

The chief tool of the microbiologist has always been the microscope. Since its

invention there have been great refinements in the optical microscope's power and precision. In addition, the electron microscope and other high-energy devices allow microbiologists to view the smallest structures of life, including the DNA molecule. However, because the powerful forms of energy that are necessary for electron microscopes, such as X-rays and particle beams, will destroy biological specimens, scientists have developed new technologies for viewing cells. The transmission electron microscope, for example, produces a shadow of the specimen by evaporating platinum metal over the viewing platform at a sharp angle. When electrons are passed through the platform at high speed, they can distinguish the shadows on the metal as a representation of the original specimen. Scanning electron microscopes, however, view the surface of a specimen by reflected radiation. In this case, the sample is also thinly coated with a heavy metal such as gold, and the biological material is observed as a cast of the more stable material. The various types of electron microscopes have allowed microbiologists to study in detail the fine structures of bacteria and viruses. With continued refinements and the development of new technologies in microscopy, it may

Electron microscopes give microbiologists the ability to view minuscule structures like chromosomes. Shutterstock.com

eventually prove possible to view individual genes or protein molecules within a cell.

Advances have also occurred in the use of pure cultures, and improvements in methods of growing and identifying microbes have found wide application in all areas of microbiology. In the laboratory, scientists must have pure cultures of microbes for their studies. If contaminating organisms are present, the

The Work of Microbiologists

Professional microbiologists are employed in a wide variety of positions. The majority work in universities, government agencies, or industry. In colleges and universities, microbiologists teach and conduct research. State and federal governments employ microbiologists to conduct research and to help regulate private-sector activities. For example, in the United States some microbiologists are employed by the federal government to inspect sewage-treatment facilities, hospitals, and food-production plants to protect the public health. Large federal agencies, such as the National Institutes of Health, the Department of Agriculture, and the Centers for Disease Control also employ microbiologists to investigate and monitor the action of microbes in our environment. There are also many commercial positions available to microbiologists. For example, wineries and breweries employ microbiologists to help standardize and maintain yeast cultures. In many other areas of industrial food production, the expertise of microbiologists is employed in quality control to guard against spoilage and contamination. Microbiologists are also employed by pharmaceutical companies to help produce vaccines and other drugs.

results of their experiments may be useless or misleading. For these reasons, microbiologists maintain pure cultures of the known microbes and provide them to associates for experimental use.

HISTORY OF MICROBIOLOGY

Microbiology began with the development of the microscope in the 17th and 18th centuries. By 1680 Anthony van Leeuwenhoek had produced a simple hand-held device that allowed scientists to view a variety of microbes in stagnant water and in scrapings from teeth. In the late 1700s Edward Jenner conducted the first vaccinations, using cowpox virus to protect people against smallpox. Later an altered form of the rabies virus was used to protect against the dreaded disease rabies. Vaccines remain the major means of protection against most viral infections.

Modern microbiology had its origins in the work of the French scientist Louis Pasteur—considered the father of microbiology—who developed methods of culturing and identifying microbes. During the second half of the 19th century, he and his contemporary Robert Koch provided final proof of the germ theory of disease. They also demonstrated that microbes must be introduced or seeded into a sterile environment and could not arise spontaneously, as had been previously believed. Pasteur was the first to propose that microbes cause chemical changes as they grow. Koch derived a central principle of modern microbiology, known as Koch's Postulate, that determines whether a particular germ causes a given disease.

Pasteur and his contemporaries developed pure culture methods for the growth of microbes. By diluting mixtures of microbes in sterile solutions, they were able to obtain droplets that contained a single microbe, which could then be grown on fresh, sterile media. In a separate procedure, they used rapid, sequential passage of cultures so that certain specimens were able to outgrow others. Thus, for the first time, stable cultures containing a single kind of microbe could be used to identify and study specific disease-causing organisms.

Another great advance in pure culture methods came in the late 19th century, when microbiologists discovered that each kind of microbe preferred a certain medium for optimal growth. Over the past century, microbiologists have made great progress in

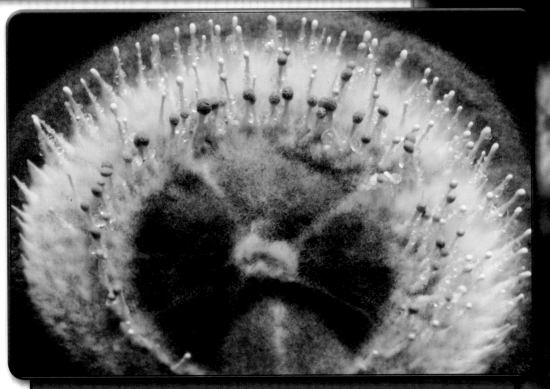

Alexander Fleming discovered that the mold Penicillium *prevents the growth of bacteria.* Hemera/Thinkstock

the preparation of selective media for the purification and identification of most species of microbes.

In 1929 Alexander Fleming observed that molds can produce a substance that prevents the growth of bacteria. His discovery, an antibiotic called penicillin, was later isolated and produced commercially to protect people against the harmful effects of certain

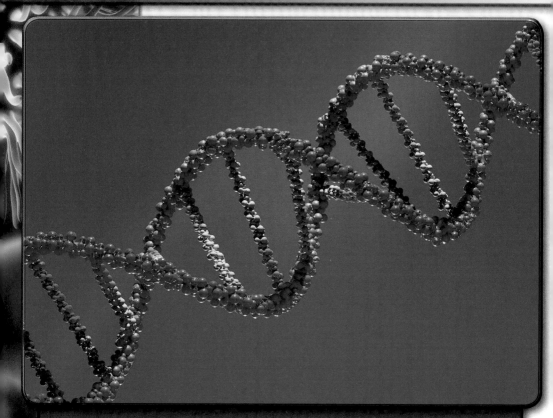

Microbiologists were able to better study the nature of DNA by using simple microbes. **Comstock/Thinkstock**

microorganisms. Today several kinds of penicillin are synthesized from various species of the mold *Penicillium* and used for different therapeutic purposes. Many other antibiotics have been identified as well, and they remain the major line of defense against infectious bacterial diseases.

In the 1940s microbiology expanded into the fields of molecular biology and genetics. Viruses were found to be simple microbes that could be studied quantitatively, and they were used to study the nature of DNA. Microbiologists began to work inside cells to study the molecular events governing the growth and development of organisms.

In the early 1970s, genetic researchers discovered recombinant DNA. Scientists found that DNA could be removed from living cells and spliced together in any combination. They were able to alter the genetic code dictating the entire structure and function of cells, tissues, and organs.

CHAPTER 4

CELL STRUCTURE AND FUNCTION

The cell is the smallest unit of living matter that can exist by itself. Some organisms, such as bacteria, consist of only a single cell. Others, such as humans and oak trees, are made up of many billions of cells.

Cells exist in a variety of shapes and sizes. Red blood cells are disk-shaped, and some skin cells resemble cubes. A single cell could be as large as a tennis ball or so small that thousands would fit on the period at the end of this sentence. Regardless of size, however, every cell contains the components needed to maintain life. Cells normally function with great efficiency, though they are vulnerable to disease.

Cell size is usually measured in microns. A micron is equal to about one millionth of a meter, and about 25,000 microns equal 1 inch. The smallest bacteria are about 0.2 micron in diameter. The diameter of the average human cell is roughly 10 microns, making it barely visible without a microscope.

All cells contain cytoplasm, a substance made up of water, proteins, and other

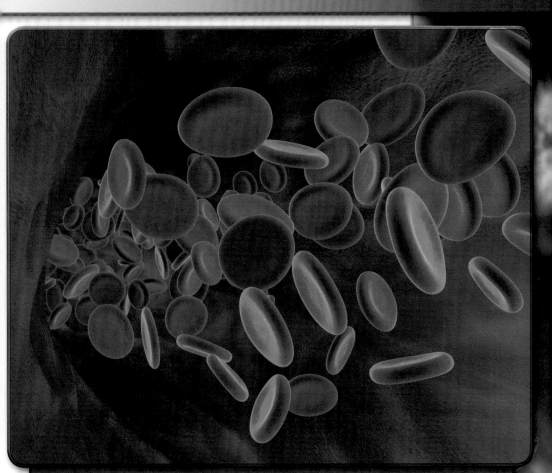

Red blood cells are shaped like disks, but other cells come in a variety of shapes and sizes. iStockphoto/Thinkstock

molecules surrounded by a membrane. The cytoplasm of eukaryotic cells also contains numerous kinds of bodies called organelles. Much of the cell's work takes place in the cytoplasm.

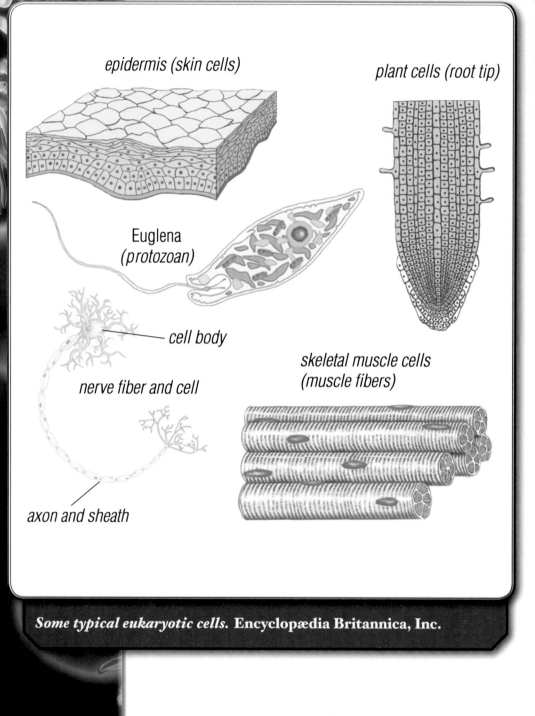

epidermis (skin cells)

plant cells (root tip)

Euglena
(protozoan)

cell body

nerve fiber and cell

skeletal muscle cells
(muscle fibers)

axon and sheath

Some typical eukaryotic cells. Encyclopædia Britannica, Inc.

PROKARYOTES AND EUKARYOTES

Based on fundamental differences in their cell structure, living organisms can be divided into two major groups: prokaryotes and eukaryotes. Bacteria and archaea are prokaryotes. Animals, plants, fungi, and protists are eukaryotes.

Prokaryotic and eukaryotic cells are distinguished by several key characteristics. Both cell types contain DNA as their genetic material. Prokaryotic DNA is single stranded and circular, however, and it floats freely inside the cell. Eukaryotic DNA is double stranded and linear and is enclosed inside a membrane-bound structure called the nucleus. Eukaryotes also have other specialized membrane-bound structures (organelles) that do much of the cell's work. Although prokaryotes lack organelles, they must accomplish many similar vital tasks. This inability to "delegate" tasks makes prokaryotes less metabolically efficient than eukaryotes.

Cell Membrane

Cells can survive only in a liquid medium that brings in food and carries away waste. For unicellular (single-celled) organisms, such as bacteria, algae, and protozoa, this fluid can be an external body of water, such as a lake or stream. For multicellular (many-celled) organisms, however, the liquid medium is contained

Sap brings in food and carries away waste in plants and trees. iStockphoto/Thinkstock

within the organism. In plants, for example, it is the sap. In animals it is the blood.

The cell membrane is semipermeable— that is, some substances can pass through it but others cannot. This characteristic enables the cell to admit or block substances from the surrounding fluid and enables the cell to excrete waste products into its environment.

The cell membrane is composed of two thin layers of phospholipid molecules studded with large proteins. Phospholipids are chemically related to fats and oils. Some membrane proteins are structural. Others form pores that function as gateways to allow or prevent the transport of substances across the membrane.

Substances pass through the cell membrane in several ways. Small uncharged molecules, such as water, pass freely down their concentration gradient (from the side of the membrane where they are in higher concentration to the side of lower concentration). This movement is called diffusion. Other materials, such as ions (charged molecules), must be transported through channels— membrane pores that are regulated by chemical signals from the cell. This facilitated transport requires energy for substances moving against a concentration gradient.

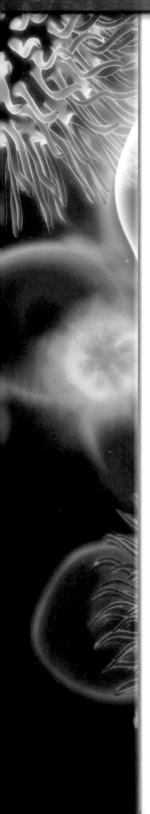

PASSIVE AND ACTIVE TRANSPORT

Substances such as glucose or ions enter the cell through specific channels, traveling down their concentration gradient. Because the process does not require energy, it is called passive transport.

Molecules moving against their concentration gradient must be "escorted" across the cell membrane. This is called active transport, and it requires the cell to spend energy. Chemical signals in the cell tell the membrane channels when to start and when to stop the transport process.

ENDOCYTOSIS AND EXOCYTOSIS

Endocytosis is a process used by cells to take in certain materials. The cell membrane forms a pocket around a substance in its environment. The filled pocket breaks loose from the membrane, forming a bubble-like vacuole that drifts into the cytoplasm, where its contents are "digested": the vacuole wall is broken down and the contents are released into the cytoplasm. The process is called pinocytosis ("pino-" is from the Greek *pinein*, meaning "to drink") when the material is dissolved in fluid and phago-cytosis ("phago-" is from the Greek *phagein*, meaning "to eat") when the cell ingests larger, particulate matter, such as another cell. The reverse process, exocytosis, is used to remove material from the cell.

CELL WALL

Virtually all prokaryotes, as well as the cells of plants, fungi, and some algae, have a cell wall—a rigid structure that surrounds the cell membrane. Most cell walls are composed of polysaccharides—long chains of sugar molecules linked by strong bonds. The cell wall helps maintain the cell's shape and, in larger organisms such as plants, enables it to grow upright. The cell wall also protects the cell against bursting under certain osmotic conditions.

Plant cell walls, as well as those of green algae and some other protists, are made mostly of the polysaccharide cellulose. In some plants, the cellulose is mixed with vary-ing amounts of other polysaccharides, such as lignin, an important component of tree bark and wood. In some fungi the cell wall is composed of chitin, a polysaccharide that

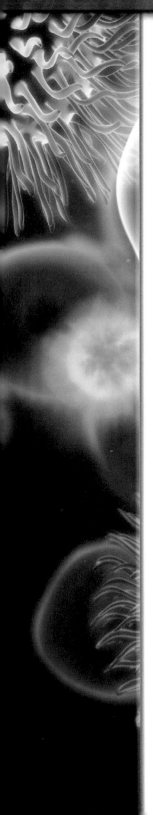

also forms the exoskeleton of many invertebrates such as insects and crabs. The bacterial cell wall is composed mostly of peptidoglycan, which is made up of polysaccharides and amino acids. The cell walls of the diatom (a tiny one-celled organism) have a high concentration of silica, which gives them a glasslike appearance.

CYTOPLASM

Water is the largest component of cytoplasm. Depending on the cell and its needs and conditions, water concentration varies from about 65 percent to roughly 95 percent. Suspended in the water are various solids such as proteins, carbohydrates, fat droplets, and pigments. As such, cytoplasm is a colloid rather than simply a solid or a liquid.

Changes in the concentration of solids produce an apparent streaming of the cytoplasm from place to place within the cell. When viewed through a microscope, membranes and fibrous structures are more readily visible in the cytoplasm when the concentration of solids increases. This visibility decreases as the solid content decreases.

ORGANELLES AND THEIR FUNCTIONS

Cells are constantly working to stay alive. Food molecules are changed into material needed for energy, and substances needed for growth and repair are synthesized, or manufactured. In eukaryotic cells most of these tasks take place inside membrane-bound bodies of the cytoplasm called organelles. According to the theory of endosymbiosis, certain organelles—in particular plastids and mitochondria—originated as small independent prokaryotic cells that invaded or were engulfed by primitive eukaryotic cells and formed an interdependent relationship with them.

PLASTIDS

Plastids are found in plant and algae cells that use photosynthesis to manufacture and store food. Chloroplasts, chromoplasts, and leucoplasts are the most common plastids. Photosynthesis takes place inside chloroplasts, which contain chlorophyll, a green pigment that captures energy from the sun and uses it to make sugar. Chromoplasts,

Chromoplasts contain pigments, such as orange carotenes and yellow xanthophylls, that create the vibrant fall colors seen in many tree species. © www.istockphoto.com/Tony Lomas

most commonly found in fruits and flower petals, contain other pigments, such as the orange carotenes, yellow xanthophylls, and red and blue anthocyanins. These pigments give fruits and flowers their colors and produce the brilliant fall hues seen in many tree species. Leucoplasts are colorless and usually contain starch granules or other materials.

All plastids have an inner and an outer membrane. The inner membrane is highly impermeable, while the outer is semipermeable. Plastids have their own DNA. It is distinct from the DNA found in the cell's nucleus and is replicated and inherited independently. Plastids manufacture some of their own proteins but rely on the cell's DNA and ribosomes to synthesize others.

MITOCHONDRIA

Often called the powerhouses of the cell, the sausage-shaped mitochondria produce the energy needed by the cell to function. Food molecules that pass into the cytoplasm are taken into the mitochondria and oxidized, or burned, for energy. Like plastids, mitochondria have an inner and an outer membrane.

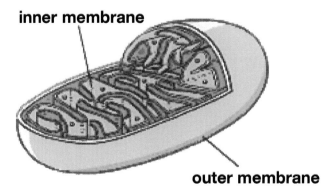

Mitochondrion

inner membrane

outer membrane

Encyclopædia Britannica Online School Edition. Copyright Encyclopædia Britannica, Inc.; rendering for this edition by Rosen Educational Services

Also like plastids, although they have their own DNA, they depend on the cell's DNA for certain proteins.

ENDOPLASMIC RETICULUM AND RIBOSOMES

The endoplasmic reticulum (ER), a network of membranous tubes and sacs, twists through the cytoplasm from the cell membrane to the membrane surrounding the nucleus. Located along portions of the

Protein Processing and Secretion

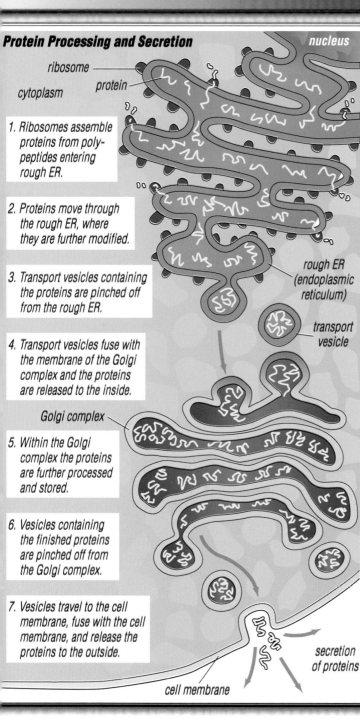

ribosome

cytoplasm

protein

nucleus

1. Ribosomes assemble proteins from polypeptides entering rough ER.

2. Proteins move through the rough ER, where they are further modified.

3. Transport vesicles containing the proteins are pinched off from the rough ER.

4. Transport vesicles fuse with the membrane of the Golgi complex and the proteins are released to the inside.

Golgi complex

5. Within the Golgi complex the proteins are further processed and stored.

6. Vesicles containing the finished proteins are pinched off from the Golgi complex.

7. Vesicles travel to the cell membrane, fuse with the cell membrane, and release the proteins to the outside.

rough ER (endoplasmic reticulum)

transport vesicle

secretion of proteins

cell membrane

The endoplasmic reticulum (ER) plays a major role in the biosynthesis of proteins. Proteins that are synthesized by ribosomes on the ER are transported into the Golgi apparatus for processing. Some of these proteins will be secreted from the cell, others will be inserted into the plasma membrane, and still others will be inserted into lysosomes. **Encyclopædia Britannica, Inc.**

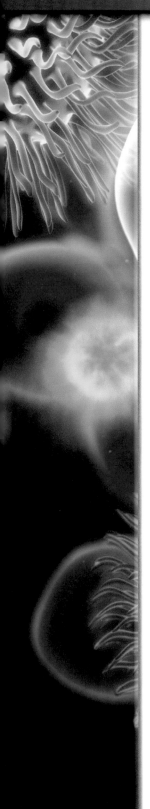

endoplasmic reticulum are ribosomes, tiny bodies made of RNA that play a vital role in the manufacture of proteins. Ribosomes are also found scattered throughout the cytoplasm; distinct sets of ribosomes are found in plastids and mitochondria.

The portions of the endoplasmic reticulum that contain ribosomes are called rough endoplasmic reticulum (RER). Areas of the network that do not contain ribosomes are called smooth endoplasmic reticulum (SER). The latter is predominant in cells involved in the synthesis and metabolism of lipids and the detoxification of some drugs.

GOLGI COMPLEX

The Golgi complex, or Golgi apparatus, is a membranous structure composed of stacks of thin sacs. Newly made proteins and lipids move from the RER and SER, respectively, to the Golgi complex. The materials are transported inside vesicles formed from the ER membrane. At the Golgi complex, the vesicles fuse with the Golgi membrane and the contents move inside the Golgi's lumen, or center, where they are further modified and subsequently stored. When the cell signals that certain proteins are needed, the latter are "packaged" by the Golgi for export— part of the Golgi membrane forms a vesicle that then buds off, or breaks away, from the larger apparatus. The vesicle may migrate to the cell membrane and export its contents via exocytosis or it may travel to an intracellular location if its contents are needed by the cell itself. Lipids are processed by the same methods.

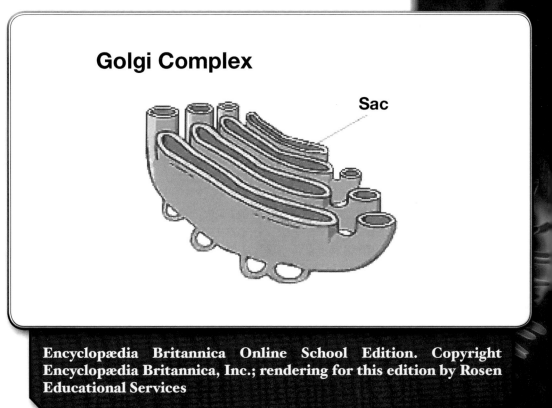

Golgi Complex

Sac

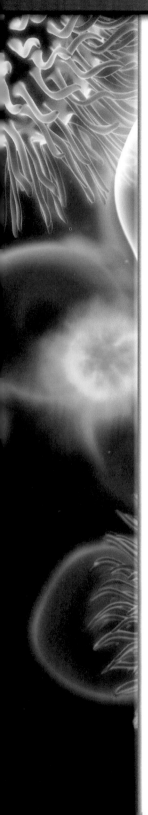

Vacuoles

Vacuoles drift through the cytoplasm and usually carry food molecules in solution. Vacuoles also regulate the water content of some single-celled organisms. For example, when an amoeba absorbs too much water, it forms a contractile vacuole against the membrane. The vacuole fills with water and then contracts to squeeze the excess liquid out of the cell.

Vacuoles in cambium cells in plants develop large central vacuoles that play a role in building stalks and stems. If a cambium cell is to become bark or wood, its membrane grows into the vacuole and deposits layers of cell wall to increase stiffness. In cells that become part of a vascular bundle that transmits sap, the vacuole becomes cylindrical and develops openings at each end that pass sap from cell to cell.

Lysosomes and Peroxisomes

Lysosomes are similar in appearance to vacuoles. Each lysosome is filled with enzymes that help the cell to digest certain materials, such as cell parts that are no longer functional, and foreign particles, such as bacteria.

Similar to lysosomes are peroxisomes, which contain enzymes that destroy toxic materials such as peroxide. Lysosomes are produced in the Golgi complex, while peroxisomes are self-replicating.

CENTROSOMES

Near the nucleus of animal, fungus, and algal cells is a spherical structure called the centrosome. Prior to the division of a cell, the centrosome divides into two centrosomes, which travel to opposite ends of the cell

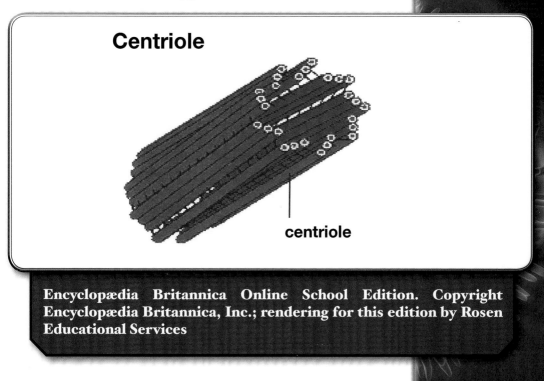

Centriole

centriole

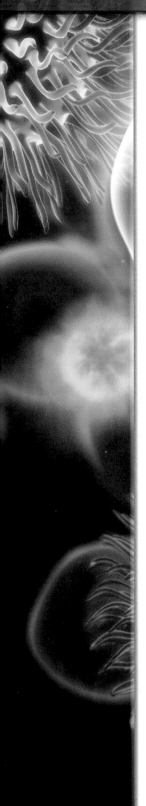

during the early phases of cell division. The centrosomes contain a pair of structures called centrioles, which produce microtubules. These protein tubes form "spindles" that extend toward the nucleus and help the cell's chromosomes separate during cell division. Plant cells lack centrioles, but they do have centrosomes, which serve a function similar to that in animal cells.

CYTOSKELETON

The cytoskeleton helps the cell maintain its shape, aids in cellular movement, and helps with internal movement. Found only in eukaryotic cells, the cytoskeleton is a network of protein filaments and tubules that extends throughout the cytoplasm. Microtubules help form structures such as cilia and flagella, which help in cell movement, and the spindle fibers that help chromosomes move during cell division. Microfilaments give the cell its shape and help it contract; intermediate filaments give it strength.

NUCLEUS

Near the middle of the cell is the nucleus. The nucleus is the control center of the cell.

It also contains the structures that transmit hereditary traits. A nucleus not undergoing division has at least one nucleolus, which is the site of RNA synthesis and storage.

The nucleus is enclosed by a two-layered membrane and contains a syrupy nucleoplasm and strands of DNA wrapped around proteins in a manner that resembles a string of beads. Each strand contains a long series of genes — segments of DNA inherited from the previous generation. Each gene determines a heritable characteristic of the organism. Genes also regulate the production of RNA, which in turn controls the manufacture of specific proteins.

The DNA strands, which are called chromatin because they readily stain with dyes, are usually too thin to be seen with an optical microscope. When a cell begins to divide, the chromatin–protein strands coil repeatedly around themselves, condensing into thicker structures called chromosomes.

How Cells Divide

Prokaryotes reproduce by several means, including simple fission (in which the cell divides after replicating its DNA) and conjugation (a form of simple sexual reproduction).

Mitosis, or Somatic Cell Division

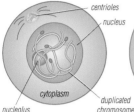

centrioles
nucleus
cytoplasm
duplicated chromosome
nucleolus

Prior to mitosis, each chromosome makes an exact duplicate of itself. The chromosomes then thicken and coil.

aster
nuclear membrane

In early prophase, the centrioles, which have divided, form asters and move apart. The nuclear membrane begins to disintegrate.

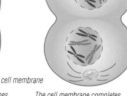

centromere
spindle fiber

In late prophase, the centrioles and asters are at opposite poles. The nucleolus and nuclear membrane have almost disappeared.

The doubled chromosomes—their centromeres attached to the spindle fibers—line up at mid-cell in the metaphase.

In early anaphase, the centromeres split. Half the chromosomes move to one pole, half to the other pole.

In late anaphase, the chromosomes have almost reached their respective poles. The cell membrane begins to pinch at the center.

cell membrane

The cell membrane completes constriction in telophase. Nuclear membranes form around the separated chromosomes.

Mitosis completed, there are two cells with the same structures and number of chromosomes as the parent cell.

One cell gives rise to two genetically identical daughter cells during the process of mitosis. **Encyclopædia Britannica, Inc.**

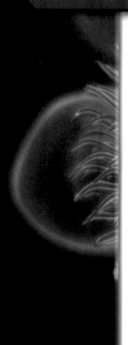

Eukaryotic cells, however, undergo a more complex division process.

The division of eukaryotic somatic cells—that is, any cell type except germ, or sex, cells—is called mitosis. Between cell divisions, each chromosome makes an exact duplicate of itself and the cell's centrosome divides in two. As mitosis begins, the nucleus signals the chromatin to condense and a body

Meiosis, or Sex Cell Division

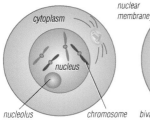

cytoplasm

nucleus

nucleolus   chromosome

At the onset of meiosis, DNA strands thicken into chromosomes. Homologous, or like, chromosomes begin to approach each other.

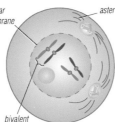

nuclear membrane   aster

bivalent

Homologous chromosomes pair to form bivalents. The centrioles divide and move to opposite poles of the cell.

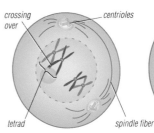

crossing over   centrioles

tetrad   spindle fiber

The bivalents duplicate to form tetrads, or four-chromatid groups. The nuclear membrane disintegrates. Crossing over (recombination) occurs.

In metaphase I, the tetrads, attached to spindle fibers at their centromeres, line up at mid-cell.

In early anaphase I, the tetrads separate, and the paired chromatids move along the spindle to their respective centrioles.

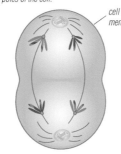

cell membrane

In late anaphase I, the chromatids have almost reached the spindle poles. The cell membrane begins to constrict.

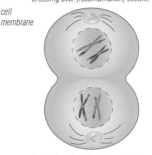

In telophase I, nuclear membranes enclose the separated chromatids. The cell membrane completes its constriction.

The first meiotic division ends. There are now two cells, each with the same number of chromatids as the parent cell.

Prophase II begins. In the second meiotic division, homologous chromatids do not duplicate but merely separate.

In metaphase II, the chromatids line up at mid-cell. The centrioles and asters are at the poles. A spindle has formed.

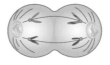

In anaphase II, the now-separated chromatids approach their respective poles. The cell membrane begins to constrict.

Telophase II has been completed. There are now four cells, each with half the number of chromosomes of the parent cell.

The formation of gametes (sex cells) occurs during the process of meiosis. Encyclopædia Britannica, Inc.

called the centromere holds each set of original and duplicate chromosomes together. The two centrosomes move to opposite ends of the cell, producing lengths of microtubules called asters and spindle fibers. The paired chromosomes become attached to individual spindle fibers and gather in a line at mid-cell. The centromeres then split, and the chromosome pairs are separated; each moves along the spindle toward its respective centrosome. Eventually, the cell divides, producing two daughter cells—each with an identical complement of chromosomes.

Each cell of a given species has a characteristic number of chromosomes. Human somatic cells normally contain 46 chromosomes—23 pairs. Mitosis ensures that both daughter cells have the full set of chromosomes characteristic of their species.

Germ cells produce gametes—sperm and eggs in humans—by meiosis. This involves two divisions. During the first division, the chromosomes pair up and duplicate themselves, sometimes exchanging genes through a process called crossing over. The first division produces two cells, each with a full set of chromosomes. During the second division, the chromosomes in the two cells do not duplicate themselves. The second division produces four gametes, each containing only one chromosome from each chromosome pair, or only half the number of chromosomes characteristic of the species. The full complement of chromosomes is restored when a male gamete combines with a female gamete. For example, a human sperm and a human egg each contain 23 chromosomes. When the sperm fertilizes the egg, the two gametes fuse, forming a cell with a complete set of 46 chromosomes. This new cell is called a zygote, and it is the beginning of a new organism.

CHAPTER 5

HISTORY OF CELL THEORY

The history of cell theory is a history of the actual observation of cells because early prediction and speculation about the nature of the cell were generally unsuccessful. The decisive event that allowed the observation of cells was the invention of the microscope in the 17th century, which stimulated interest in the "invisible" world.

FORMULATION OF THE THEORY

Robert Hooke, who described cork and other plant tissues in 1665, introduced the term "cell" because the cellulose walls of dead cork cells reminded him of the blocks of cells occupied by monks. Even after the publication in 1672 of excellent pictures of plant tissues, no significance was attached to the contents within the cell walls. The magnifying powers of the microscope and the inadequacy of techniques for preparing cells for observation precluded a study of the intimate details of the cell contents. Beginning in 1673,

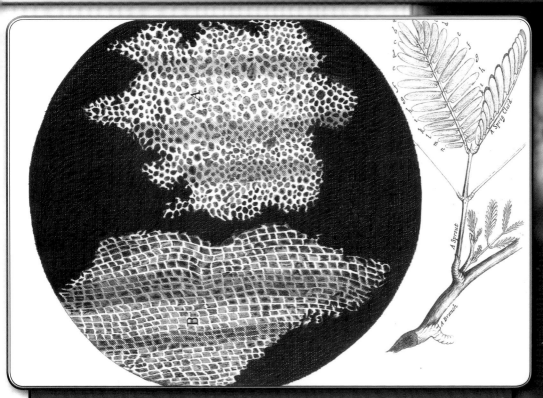

The cellulose walls of dead cork cells reminded Robert Hooke of monks' cells. **SSPL via Getty Images**

Anthony van Leeuwenhoek discovered blood cells, spermatozoa, and a lively world of "animalcules." A new world of unicellular organisms was opened up. Such discoveries extended the known variety of living things but did not bring insight into their basic uniformity. Moreover, when Leeuwenhoek observed the swarming of his animalcules but failed to observe their division,

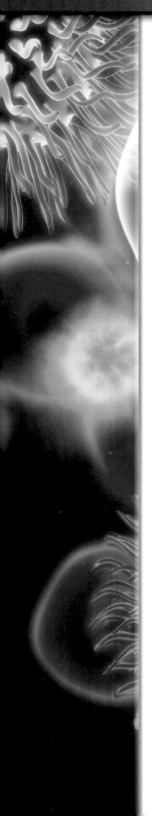

he could only reinforce the idea that they arose spontaneously.

Cell theory was not formulated for nearly 200 years after the introduction of microscopy. Explanations for this delay range from the poor quality of the microscopes to the persistence of ancient ideas concerning the definition of a fundamental living unit. Many observations of cells were made, but apparently none of the observers could assert forcefully that cells are the units of biological structure and function.

Three critical discoveries made during the 1830s, when improved microscopes with suitable lenses, higher powers of magnification, and more satisfactory illumination became available, were decisive events in the early development of cell theory. First, the nucleus was observed by Scottish botanist Robert Brown in 1833 as a constant component of plant cells. Next, nuclei were also observed and recognized as such in some animal cells. Finally, a living substance called protoplasm was recognized within cells, its vitality made evident by its active streaming, or flowing, movements, especially in plant cells. After these three discoveries, cells, previously considered as mere pores in plant tissue, could no longer be thought of as empty, because they contained living material.

German physiologist Theodor Schwann and German biologist Matthias Schleiden clearly stated in 1839 that cells are the "elementary particles of organisms" in both plants and animals and recognized that some organisms are unicellular and others multicellular. Schleiden and Schwann's descriptive statements concerning the cellular basis of biologic structure are straightforward and acceptable to modern thought. They recognized the common features of cells to be the membrane, nucleus, and cell body and described them in comparisons of various animal and plant tissues.

Matthias Schleiden. **Kean Collection/Archive Photos/Getty Images**

THE PROBLEM OF THE ORIGIN OF CELLS

Schwann and Schleiden were not alone in contributing to this great generalization of natural science. Strong intimations of the cell theory occur in the work of their predecessors. Recognizing that the basic problem was the origin of cells, these early investigators invented a hypothesis of "free cell formation," according to which cells developed out of an unformed substance, a "cytoblastema," by a sequence of events in which first the nucleolus develops, followed by the nucleus, the cell body, and finally the cell membrane. Even though cell division was observed repeatedly in the following decades, the theory of free cell formation lingered throughout most of the 19th century. However, it came to be thought of more and more as a possible exception to the general principle of the reproduction of cells by division. The correct general principle was affirmed in 1855 by a German scientist, Rudolph Virchow, who asserted that "omnis cellula e cellula" ("all cells come from cells").

The inherently complex events of cell division prevented a quick resolution of the complete sequence of changes that occur during the process. First, it was noted that a

Rudolph Virchow. **Courtesy of Bildarchiv Preussischer Kulturbesitz BPK, Berlin**

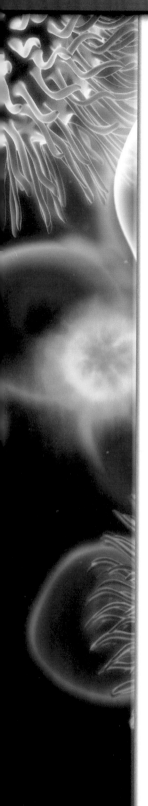

cell with a nucleus divides into two cells, each having a nucleus. Hence, it was concluded that the nucleus must divide, and direct division of nuclei was correctly described by some. Better techniques created some confusion, because it was found that during cell division the nucleus as such disappears. Also, at the time of division, dimly observed masses, now recognized as chromosomes, were seen to appear temporarily. Observations in the 1870s culminated in the highly accurate description and interpretation of cell division by German anatomist Walther Flemming in 1882. His advanced techniques of fixing and staining cells enabled him to see that cell reproduction involves the transmission of chromosomes from the parent to daughter cells by the process of mitosis and that the division of the cell body is the concluding event of that reproduction.

The discovery that the number of chromosomes remains constant from one generation to the next resulted in the full explanation of the process of meiosis. The description of meiosis, combined with the observation that fertilization is fundamentally the union of maternal and paternal sets of chromosomes, resulted in the understanding of the physical basis of reproduction and heredity.

Rudolph Virchow

One of the most prominent physicians of the 19th century, German scientist and statesman Rudolph Virchow pioneered the modern concept of the pathological processes of disease. He emphasized that diseases did not arise in organs or tissues in general but primarily in individual cells. Virchow also contributed to the development of anthropology as a modern science.

Rudolph Carl Virchow was born on Oct. 13, 1821, in Schivelbein, Prussia. He studied at the University of Berlin and graduated as a doctor of medicine in 1843. As a young intern, Virchow published a paper on one of the two earliest reported cases of leukemia. His paper became a classic. In 1849 Virchow was appointed to the chair of pathological anatomy at the University of Würzburg—the first chair of that subject in Germany. In 1856 Virchow became director of the Pathological Institute at the University of Berlin.

Virchow's concept of cellular pathology replaced the existing theory that disease arose from an imbalance of the four fluid humors of the body: blood, phlegm, yellow bile, and black bile. He applied the cell theory to disease processes and stated that diseased cells arose from preexisting diseased cells. In 1859 Virchow was elected to the Berlin City Council on which he dealt mainly with such public health matters as sewage disposal, the design of hospitals, meat inspection, and school hygiene. He also designed the new Berlin sewer system. Virchow was elected to the Prussian National Assembly in 1861 and to the German Reichstag in 1880.

Virchow's work in pathological anatomy had led him to begin anthropological work with studies of skulls. He was the organizer of German anthropology, and in 1869 he founded the Berlin Society for Anthropology, Ethnology, and Prehistory. Virchow died on Sept. 5, 1902, in Berlin, Germany.

Meiosis and fertilization therefore came to be understood as the complementary events in the life cycle of organisms: meiosis halves the number of chromosomes in the formation of spores (plants) or gametes (animals), while fertilization restores the number through the union of gametes. By the 1890s "life" in all of its manifestations could be thought of as an expression of cells.

CONCLUSION

During the 20th century, biology changed from a predominantly descriptive science to one keenly founded on experimentation and deductive reasoning. Discoveries such as using antibiotics to treat infectious disease and insulin to treat diabetes, as well as increased knowledge about cell development, were among the many important advances made over the past 100 years or so.

In the early 21st century, genetics and molecular biology have been two of the most active areas of biological research. In 2003, exactly 50 years after British biophysicist Francis Crick and American geneticist James Watson described the double-helical structure of DNA, the Human Genome Project was completed. The 13-year international collaboration of more than 2,800 researchers—one of the boldest scientific undertakings in history—identified all of the approximately 25,000 human genes and determined the sequences of the 3 billion chemical base pairs that make up human

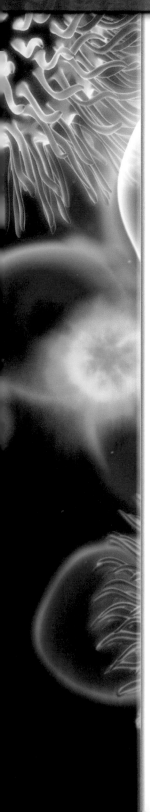

DNA. The genetic information provided by the project has enabled researchers to pinpoint errors in genes that cause or contribute to disease. In the future, having the tools to know the precise genetic makeup of individuals will enable health care providers to deliver truly personalized medicine.

animalcule A tiny, usually microscopic, organism.

archaea Microorganisms of the domain Archaea similar in structure to bacteria that include methane-producing forms and others of harsh, hot, acidic, or otherwise extreme environments.

chromosome A microscopic, threadlike part of the cell that carries hereditary information in the form of genes.

contractile vacuole Membrane-like sac within single-celled organisms (like amoebae and other protozoans) that fills with water and suddenly contracts, expelling its contents from the cell.

glean To gather information or material bit by bit.

heritable Able to be inherited or passed on from parent to offspring.

indefinite Not certain or limited (as in amount or length); having no exact limits.

insidious Having a more harmful effect than is apparent.

media A nourishing system for the artificial cultivation of microorganisms or cells.

morphology The form and structure of a plant or animal or any of its parts.

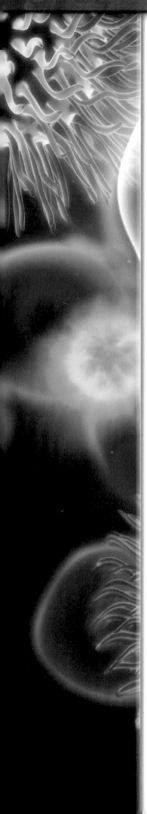

nucleotide Any of a class of organic compounds, including the structural units of nucleic acids.

oxidize To combine with oxygen; to remove hydrogen from, especially by the action of oxygen.

perplexity The state of being puzzled or filled with uncertainty; bewilderment.

phospholipid A type of lipid found in all living cells in which phosphoric acid and a fatty acid are converted to glycerol.

phylogenetic Based on natural evolutionary relationships; acquired in the course of evolutionary development.

protoplasm Usually transparent jellylike substance within a cell.

protozoa Any of a phylum or subkingdom (Protozoa) of chiefly motile and heterotrophic unicellular protists (as amoebas) that are represented in almost every kind of habitat and include some disease-causing parasites of humans and domestic animals.

recombinant Relating to or containing genetically engineered DNA.

solvent A usually liquid substance capable of dissolving one or more other substances.

spermatozoa A motile male sex cell of an animal usually with rounded or elongated head and a long posterior flagellum.

spindle Structure made up of protein fibers that is formed in the cytoplasm during cell division.

synthesis The combination of parts or elements to form a whole.

tenet A widely held belief; especially one held in common by members of a group or profession.

unprecedented Having no earlier occurrence; original.

vacuole A small cavity or space in the tissues of an organism containing air or fluid.

vesicle A small cavity, cyst, or blister usually filled with fluid.

FOR MORE INFORMATION

American Society for Microbiology
1752 N Street
Washington, DC 20036-2904
(202) 737-3600
Web site: http://www.asm.org
The central organization of microbiologists in
the United States provides information, cur-
rent microbiology news, and and resources
for students interested in microbiology.

Bamfield Marine Sciences Centre
100 Pachena Rd
Bamfield, BC V0R 1B0
Canada
(250) 728-3301
Web site: http://www.oceanlink.info
A variety of resources are available from
Canada's premier coastal and marine
facility for teaching and research.

Center for Bioethics
285 Mercer Street, 9th Floor
New York, NY 10003
(212) 998-8329
Web site: http://bioethics.as.nyu.edu/
page/home
A program within New York University
that focuses on bioethics education and
awareness.

Microbes in Action program
University of Missouri
One University Boulevard
St. Louis, MO 63121-4400
Web site: http://www.umsl.edu/~microbes/
   index.html
This program is run through University of
   Missouri's biology program. The goal is
   to encourage education and appreciation
   of the role of microorganisms. It provides
   resources, information, and hands-on
   activities relating to microbiology.

National Museum of Natural History
P.O. Box 37012 Smithsonian Inst.
Washington, DC 20013-7012
Web site: http://www.mnh.si.edu
The National Museum of Natural History is
   a part of the Smithsonian Institution, a
   world-renowned, state-of-the-art research
   center and museum. Students can visit
   the site or the museum to investigate a
   wide variety of natural history topics.

Nature Canada
75 Albert Street, Suite 300
Ottawa, ON K1P 5E7
Canada
(800) 267-4088

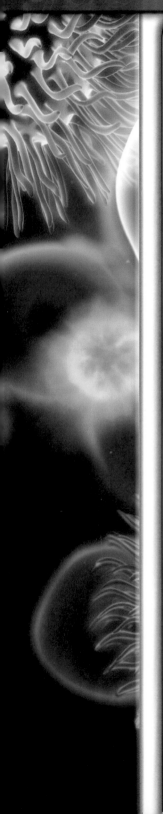

Web site: http://www.naturecanada.ca

Nature Canada seeks to protect wildlife and natural habitats throughout Canada. Outreach programs, publications, and volunteer support are the primary means the organization uses to reach its goals.

Virginia Institute of Marine Sciences
PO Box 1346
Rt. 1208 Greate Road
Gloucester Point, VA 23062-1346
(804) 684-7000
Web site: http://www.vims.edu

The institute, based out of the College of William and Mary, is both a research and educational institution on oceans and the study of its systems. It provides internships, public programs, and advanced research programs.

WEB SITES

Due to the changing nature of Internet links, Rosen Educational Services has developed an online list of Web sites related to the subject of this book. This site is updated regularly. Please use this link to access the list:

http://www.rosenlinks.com/biol/bmtc

Alberts, Bruce, and others. *Essential Cell Biology*, 3rd ed. (Garland Science, 2009).

Betsy, Tom, and Keogh, James Edward. *Microbiology Demystified* (McGraw-Hill, 2005).

Cohen, Marina. *Cells* (Crabtree, 2010).

Hoagland, Mahlon, and others. *Exploring the Way Life Works: The Science of Biology* (Jones & Bartlett, 2001).

Kramer, Stephen. *Hidden Worlds: Looking Through a Scientist's Microscope* (Houghton Mifflin, 2001).

Morgan, Sally. *Cells and Cell Function* (Heinemann Library, 2006).

Purves, William, and others. *Life: The Science of Biology*, 7th ed. (W.H. Freeman, 2004).

Robinson, Richard, ed. *Biology* (Macmillan Reference, 2002).

Stewart, Melissa. *Cell Biology* (Twenty-First Century Books, 2008).

Tocci, Salvatore. *Biology Projects for Young Scientists*, rev. ed. (Watts, 2000).

INDEX

A

anatomy, 19

B

bacteriology, 40
bioethics, 18
biological classification,
    33–34
biological warfare, 43
biology
    about, 10–11
    areas of study in, 10–25
    history of, 26–37
    modern developments,
        36–37
botany, 29–30
Brown, Robert, 78

C

cell division, 70, 71–75,
    77–78, 80–82
cell membrane, 56–59, 79
    and endocytosis and
        exocytosis, 58–59, 67
    passive and active
        transport, 58
cell structure and func-
    tion, 52–75
cell theory, history of,
    76–84
    formulation of theory,
        76–79

problem of origin of
    cells, 80–84
cell wall, 59–60
centrosomes, 69–70
cloning, 16, 17
Crick, Francis, 85
cytoplasm, 52–53, 58,
    60, 61, 63, 64, 66,
    68, 70
cytoskeleton of cell, 70

D

Darwin, Charles, 34–35
developmental biology,
    16–17
DNA
    discovery of structure
        of, 36–37, 85
    recombinant, 21–22, 51

E

ecology, 22
embryology, 16–17
endoplasmic reticulum,
    64–66
ethology, 22–23
eukaryotes, 41, 53, 55, 61,
    70, 72
evolutionary biology,
    24–25
evolutionary theory, 15,
    34–35, 36
exobiology, 42–43

F

Fleming, Alexander, 49
Flemming, Walther, 82

G

genetic engineering, 20,
    21–22
genetics, 19–20, 35–36, 37, 51
Golgi complex, 66–67, 69
Greeks and natural law,
    26–28

H

heredity, mechanism of,
    35–36
Hooke, Robert, 33, 76
Human Genome Project,
    85–86

J

Jenner, Edward, 47

K

Koch, Robert, 47–48
Koch's Postulate, 48

L

Leeuwenhoek, Anthony
    van, 31, 32–33, 47, 77–78

Linnaean system of
    classification, 13–15,
    33–34
Linnaeus, Carolus, 13, 33
lysosomes, 68–69

M

meiosis, 74–75, 82, 84
Mendel, Gregor, 35–36
microbiology, 38–51
    areas of study, 40–43
    history of, 47–51
    methods of, 43–47
    work of microbiolo-
        gists, 46
microscopes, 43–44, 78
    development of, 31, 32,
        47, 76
    electron, 44
Middle Ages, study of
    biology in, 28
mitochondria, 61,
    63–64, 66
mitosis, 72–74, 82
molecular biology, 19–20,
    37, 51
morphology, 19
mycology, 41

N

natural selection, 34–35
nucleus of cell, 70–71, 78,
    79, 82

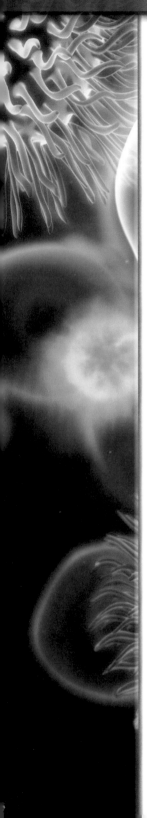

O

organelles, 53, 55, 61–70

P

Pasteur, Louis, 47–48
penicillin, 49–50
peroxisomes, 69
phycology, 41
physiology, 19
plastids, 61–63, 64, 66
prokaryotes, 55, 59, 61, 71
protozoology, 40–41
pure cultures, 45–47,
    48–49

R

Renaissance, study of
    biology during, 28–30
ribosomes, 66

S

Schleiden, Matthias, 79, 80
Schwann, Theodor, 79, 80
sociobiology, 22–23
stem cell research, 16–17

T

taxonomy, 13–16

V

vaccines, 46, 47
vacuoles, 68
Virchow, Rudolph, 80, 83
virology, 41–42

W

Wallace, Alfred Russel, 34
Watson, James, 85